LOOKING FOR THE FUTURE

ALSO BY LESLIE DUNBAR

A Republic of Equals (1966)

*A Minority Report: What Has Happened to Blacks, Hispanics,
American Indians, and other Minorities in the Eighties* (1984)

*The Common Interest: How Our Social-Welfare Policies
Don't Work and What We Can Do About Them* (1988)

Reclaiming Liberalism (1991)

The Shame of Southern Politics: Essays and Speeches (2002)

LOOKING FOR THE FUTURE

A Meditation on Political Choice

❀

LESLIE DUNBAR

NEWSOUTH BOOKS
Montgomery

NewSouth Books
105 S. Court Street
Montgomery, AL 36104

Library of Congress Cataloging-in-Publication Data

Dunbar, Leslie.
Looking for the future : a meditation on political choice / Leslie Dunbar.

p. cm.

Includes bibliographical references.

ISBN 978-1-60306-201-5 (alk. paper) — ISBN 1-60306-201-7 (alk. paper)

1. United States—Politics and government. 2. Politics and war—United States.
3. Divided government—United States. 4. Social choice—United States.
I. Title.
JK31.D86 2012
320.973—dc23

2012013106

Printed in the United States of America

FOR OUR BELOVED LINDA

AND, ALWAYS, FOR PEGGY

A writer one can learn much from is the philosopher Alfred North Whitehead. He also had the gift of writing prose sentences that read like a string of aphorisms and thus are often memorable. In one book he wrote: "The vigor of civilized societies is preserved by the widespread sense that high aims are worth-while." That is, many believers in "high aims" can be a social dynamo.

Journalist Walter Lippmann, widely listened to from the 1930s through the '70s, whom I shall be quoting at length, warned about having too-high aims that can crush the spirits of many. He gave examples, such as in our country the let-down in civic spirit following the exuberance of the 1960s. But what if any "high aiming" are we doing in this current era of self-enriching and of continuous warring—often against imagined foreign enemies?

Whitehead went on to say: "Each age deposits its message as to the secret character of the nature of things. Civilization can only be understood by those who are civilized . . . [The] great periods of history act as an enlightenment. They reveal ourselves to ourselves."

Trying to think about this is why I have called this book a meditation.

— L. D.

CONTENTS

1

The Four Horsemen

Militarism, the Church, Oligarchy, the South

I have lived most of my life up and down and sideways in our Eastern states and reside now in the venerable city of New Orleans on Magazine Street, so-called because its one-time French occupiers used its buildings as warehouses, especially for exports, which is still a recognizable English meaning of "magazines." I suppose we could stretch that definition to include the warehousing of those national ideas and ideals which we have determinedly claimed to be good and justifying our world mission.

The wars of the twentieth and twenty-first centuries have, it seems to me, tragically militarized that mission. The ideas and values we are engaged in exporting in this century and in the preceding one seem all too often to encourage fighting or the preparation for it.

I have little if anything to add to what has been said by numerous others throughout the centuries in behalf of "a better way" of conducting international relations. Later in this book I contend that there is little likelihood of progress toward a more peaceful way of social life as long as we follow the age-old practice of exaggeratedly honoring military men and women and the values they represent. Civilization is the result of the ideals and purposes people have created in their histories. It is time to withdraw the high valuation that nearly all peoples have accorded martial behaviors. Until we do, or at least greatly lower them, wars and aggressions will go on: where the honors may be, men will seek them.

Another theme of this book is the need to reject war as a guiding national principle. For that it is worth looking back at our wars. Ask for a start how they contributed to our security, to making our nation "more safe." What added national security did we gain by the Korean War, by the long dreadful Vietnam War, by our "invasion" of Grenada, by our attempted stranglehold of Cuba, and by our wars whose purpose was defined by vague theories of national security such as Kuwait, Iraq, and Afghanistan, and more lately Libya. The American peace movement, such as it is, opposed every single one of these; it must tire these champions of peace, being consistently right.

ONE YEAR MY WIFE and I went on an Elderhostel trip to Ireland. Elder-hostels always include "free days," and on one of those I detached myself from our group and went on my own wandering, sure that the street map in my hands would guide me to our eventual planned meeting place at a pub near the Abbey Theatre. But alas, my map reading was producing worrisome and unexpected sights. Spotting an accommodating-looking gentleman at a street corner, I asked for help with my map in hand.

"Well, sir, the fact is that you are going in just the wrong direction. You best turn 'round." He then told me the way. "But sir, don't be put out with yourself for what you have done. Just think of all the interest-ing things you have seen that you would have missed if you had gone the right way."

My life has been full of wrong-turnings, and some misadventures have turned out happily as did that one. I believe this has been so because our world has an endless supply of good roads to take, sights to marvel over, beauties to see and hear, and challenging jobs to do. It is a world full of beauty, natural and man-made. More beauty, I like to believe, than even the piles of ugly things also created by men, addicted as we are to befouling our mutual homes and killing each other.

And so a third theme of the book is the need to heal fissures that undermine our sense of nation, and what our South's special history teaches us about this. In the summer of 1958, I joined the staff of the Atlanta-based Southern Regional Council, then the South's strongest interracial organization committed to racial equality and justice. The Council, though small by most measures, was then under the leadership of a top-grade man, Harold C. Fleming. I worked there until 1965. These were among the South's years of terror and hate as observed by the world's peoples. Those of us who viewed from up close were also able to observe some of the worst of human potential. More memorably, we saw the greatness and goodness that we also share.

It was a transformative period for the South and also for America in its every part. Not everything changed, however. Politically, the region began the mid-1950s nearly suffocated by rebellion against our Constitutional law. It had turned to what its leaders called "massive resistance" and practiced that in extremely violent ways. Several decades later, with leadership drawn from essentially the same Southern white social and political class, it is again resistant to the national will, but this time with allies stretching from Alaska to our Southwest and in-between. Our constitutional democracy seems to have as many foes as friends. This era's "massive resisters" are different from but perhaps a more formidable threat to national unity than were those of the 1950s and 1960s.

THEN THERE IS THE Christian church. Its modern American form includes large, and growing larger, evangelical congregations, most of which appear to have little or no respect for, or even awareness of, the tradition of separation of church and state; there is sometimes actual repudiation of that belief. The centuries of theological study and debate, that did so much to create the modern mind and its openness to science and democracy, are left behind as impediments to the new spirit of a modern church that often seems to be identifying religion with American pride.

The evangelicals are ironically now in close working alliance with many Roman Catholic congregations, those who despite their deep and deeply honored traditions of witnessing for world peace and identification with the poor and the oppressed are now emphasizing above-all certain rigid sexual standards. And now we see these evangelicals and Protestant and Roman Catholic hierarchies linked in political relationships with wealthy Mormons. Modernity is besieged.

I begin by a first look at the warriors and the churches.

2

The Warriors

There is a place in *Intruder in the Dust*, one of William Faulkner's more widely read novels, when he writes:

> It's all *now* you see. Yesterday won't be over until tomorrow and tomorrow began ten thousand years ago. For every Southern boy fourteen years old, not once but whenever he wants it, there is the instant when it's still not yet two o'clock on that July afternoon in 1863, the brigades are in position behind the rail fence, the guns are laid and ready in the woods and the furled flags are already loosened to break out and Pickett himself with his long oiled ringlets and his hat in one hand probably and his sword in the other looking up the hill waiting for Longstreet to give the word and it's all in the balance, it hasn't happened yet, it hasn't even begun yet, it not only hasn't begun yet but there is still time for it not to begin against that position and those circumstances which made more men than Garnett and Kemper and Armistead and Wilcox look grave yet it's going to begin, we all know that, we have come too far with too much at stake and that moment doesn't need even a fourteen-year-old boy to think *This time. Maybe this time* with all this much to lose than all this much to gain: Pennsylvania, Maryland, the world, the golden dome of Washington itself to crown with desperate and unbelievable victory the desperate gamble, the cast made two years ago; . . .

Faulkner's inward look here into Southern minds was also a looking away from many thousand Negro lads, and maybe about the same number of poor white boys, few of whom were likely dreaming of a better outcome at Gettysburg. Faulkner did see them more clearly in other novels. What he was, however, locating in *Intruder* was the tragic romance that was to come from those battlefields, and he saw that it would linger at the core of too many Southern minds.

Even today and despite substantial in-migration from other regions and countries it has not let go. The romance of it helped fix as honored figures in our minds, our societies, and political structures "the warriors." *The Warrior.* The higher the rank of the warrior the more honor received.

I have not read widely or deeply into Civil War biographies. They are mostly of the battlefield leaders, and those are not my heroes or teachers. Respected historians and literary critics do, however, recommend Ulysses S. Grant's book. Perhaps I should read it, for it might rid me of my reluctance to speak with full reverence of Lincoln, Grant's chief. There must have been a better way to free the slaves, I keep thinking, than the killing fields that the Civil War became.

There must have been a better way to free the slaves, if only we could have thought of it! In another of his Civil War-related books, *The Unvanquished* (the name itself seems a battle cry), Faulkner wonders if women might have known the better way. But of the two heroines of this novel, one contrived to steal the Yankee soldiers' mules and then, in a hilarious telling, sell them back to the Union army; and the other heroine disguised herself as a man in order to join the army and "kill Yankees" as her fiancée had done before he died in battle at Shiloh. As Kurt Vonnegut might say, "So it goes."

A major political problem with which this essay is concerned is the warrior class that penetrates and in growing measure directs our American society. The same class directs the political choices of most other countries, too.

By that name "warrior class" I include all those uniformed persons, of all nations, who make their living by killing, or being prepared to kill, enemies of their nations. Their governments have selected this class, and it is set apart from their countrymen by recognized privileges. Also in this class I include those civilians who for hire plan, manage, carry out, and thereby profit (often greatly) from military actions.

The vastness of big national governments and their characteristic complexity makes difficult a narrower definition of the class. The ability to make war against others and to respond when other governments make wars against us has been for centuries the accepted primary duty and purpose of states and their governments; the warriors are a society's vanguard.

Most people, I not quite resignedly suppose, would believe that that is as it should be. If most people are right, those who are opposed to war have to devise institutions and processes that can trustworthily postpone or lessen the destructiveness of the fighting. Many fine proposals to that end have been made over long centuries. Most people would and will think it right for the warrior class to be the fundament of our ruling class because the opinion of those same "most people" throughout the ages has been that the primary purpose of government is the protection from foes.

From the time of St. Augustine or earlier, ethicists, theologians, and just plain thoughtful women and men have questioned why war has been institutionalized for, as it seems, often base purposes.[1] Great essays have been written, going back at least as far as Immanuel Kant's *Perpetual Peace*. I would like to add to them merely another topic, one that has been too little emphasized and perhaps an overly naive one. It has the advantage, however, of not asking any government's support.

The proposal is simply this: stop honoring military service so extravagantly. It is ironic, is it not, that the Christian churches have, over the centuries, adopted and often vigorously championed newer and certainly non-Biblical social commitments—such as against slavery, racial segregation, anti-Semitism, and capital punishment, none of which is much if at all in Scripture—while widely forsaking ancient commitments that were declared or strongly implied there: principally, those against war and for the rights of the poor.

War is, of course, the chief concern of the state. That is still true, is it not, in this era of war without end? How routinely do we tell ourselves that "national security" is the most important social, even ethical, value? Yet when did it become a goal of the church?

That original devotion of the early Christian church to the downtrodden and afflicted, and to the lion lying down with the lamb, set it at odds with virtually every then-existent state including, of course, its home state, the Roman Empire. May it have been, and is it still, that the price of Christianity's eventual toleration by the Empire, and its multitude of successor state powers, was the yielding of those birthright commitments to peacefulness and to the poor? The "just war" theory grew from that yielding; the church, to be respected and in some states even tolerated, had to be and has to be a "patriot church."

We have heard a lot of the "just war" theory, especially since the first president Bush asserted it in defense of war against Iraq in the early 1990s. It had been enunciated in the fifth century by St. Augustine and moderately refined about eight hundred years later by other churchmen, including St. Thomas of Aquinas. Its use has been pretty well confined to the strengthening of a government's case for a war decided on. It has rarely been invoked as a reason not to start one. It always supports the affirmative side of the debate when the question is, "Shall war be approved?"

Besides, what government, intent on warring, ever fails to claim that it is legally empowered to judge the necessity of military force, that the enemy has done wrong, and that its own purposes and methods are good—these being the essential requirements of a "just war"—and that therefore to go to war is rightful. It is hard for religion, especially for a patriotic church, to combat such claims.

3

OUR MILITARIZED AGE AND SOCIETY

There is scant military tradition in my family. My father was born in 1875. He had been either too young or too old for the Spanish-American War, the Great War, and World War II, and the Indian wars on the frontier probably required more spirit of militancy than reached into the fastness of the West Virginia mountains that were our family's home.

It has been a source of amazement to me that I had a grandfather born in 1829, when Andrew Jackson was in his first term. But his military record was also not spectacular. Family records do say that early in the Civil War my grandfather Dunbar was elected captain of a militia company which was directed by the Virginia government to march to an ongoing engagement near Little Sewell Mountain. But when they arrived, the campaign was over. Both Generals Rosecrans and Lee had withdrawn without a final fight. The members of the company went home to Greenbrier County, were mustered out, and did not pick up their guns again. Theirs had not been a particularly exciting service. Whether their action or non-action reflected a dislike of the Civil War, of war in general, or of the State of Virginia, from which its western counties withdrew a year later, I have no idea.

We were always Democrats, and when at my age of eight several economic forces and reversals of fortune drove my family to move to Baltimore, we carried that political alliance with us. As a child I had been fond of a big red book about the World War that was in our house, and I knew the names and looks of Pershing, Foch, and other World War I heroes and German "villains." However, growing through my teens I learned of the horror side of that merciless war and was myself absorbed in the controversies of the 1930s, the New Deal here and the emergence of Fascism dominating them all. I was not, however, what has come to be called an "activist" (a word I have always disliked), and my support on campuses, both high school and college, for President Roosevelt was strong.

So, my personally fateful resistance to ROTC, two years of which was required of male students at the University of Maryland, was not really principled. I just was drawn more to my home and dinner forty miles away than I was to memorizing the ROTC primer. As a result, in my senior year I had to retake ROTC because I had failed two earlier semesters. I managed to pass one of them but would not believe, like any undergraduate, that my graduation was at stake, and when notified by the dean's office a fortnight or so before the end of term that indeed it was, I borrowed from a classmate a copy of the text book (I had never had one of my own), almost memorized the relevant pages, got a flat 100 on the final exam, and relaxed. A couple of days before commencement I was called and informed that I was still, by a factor of two points, short of the passing grade of 70—I had cut one drill too many. A weekend of pleading was unavailing, my family had little standing, and so despite the yearbook's showing me as graduating in the class of 1941, I did not, and I have no AB degree.

That two-point deficit had its own story. Earlier in that Spring of 1941 I had seen an announcement by the Glenn L. Martin Company of job openings at its aircraft plant in Middle River, Maryland. I had made no plans yet for work after graduation; but because I was sure that war was imminent and thought I might as well get started at it, I sent in an application. I got back a job offer and a starting date. This was totally unexpected. With youthful ardor and stupidity I accepted and went to work as a trainee—the actual term used was "clerk"—in the Subcontracting Department's night shift. Thus my last undergraduate weeks combined study with a nightly occupation. I had never been able to afford living on campus and had commuted daily by carpooling or hitchhiking (for which, I guess my ROTC uniform was a useful asset) from our home in Baltimore to the College Park campus. One morning too many, I just could not do it and one-too-many ROTC drills was thus missed.

Glenn L. Martin was an antecedent through a few corporate muta-
tions of the present-day Lockheed Martin. We built several types of planes
during the war, and mine was always the medium bomber, the B-26. I
believe that there are opinions that it proved in battle to be a lesser plane
than the B-25, made by another company, but we produced a lot of them,
about a couple of thousand. I seemed to do my job well, and was gone
from that night shift fairly quickly. I advanced to a supervisory level.

I was then falling deeply in love with the young woman who became my wife for sixty-seven years. Notwithstanding that I sought to
enlist. Thus I reported to the Fifth Regiment Armory in Baltimore for
induction. All went well, until after sitting and waiting for my swearing
in and the ensuing bus ride to Camp Meade, I was at last called into a
room where I was, to my consternation and disbelief, told I was physically unfit, which I strongly resented. It seems I had a "spot" on a lung.
Family doctors whom I later consulted theorized that the calcified spot
might have been the mark left by an earlier severe bout of pneumonia.
It was painful. I wanted to be with my generation.

Yet I had the sincere idea that by doing my job I was making a con-
tribution to the war effort. So I had neither a college degree nor an Army
experience. By dint of some hard work I later nevertheless qualified for
graduate studies, and by 1948 held both an MA and a PhD from Cornell
University. I had embarked on an academic career.

First step, teaching political science at Emory. I departed after three
years, however, because the Korean and then the Cold War created openings for one with a degree in political science. Of equal importance, a
growing family could not get along well on the salary of an assistant
professor. So I applied for a job with the Air Force in "target research,"
based in Washington, to be schooled in matters Russian. The job came
through and I accepted it but on its heels so did an administrative position with the Atomic Energy Commission at its Savannah River Plant
then under construction in the region of Augusta, Georgia, and Aiken,
South Carolina. My wife and I much preferred the South over living and
working in Washington. So there I was, again in the munitions business,
this time making bombs and not planes, but having even less to do with

the actual product. The Savannah River Plant was at that time seen as the American response to the USSR's mastery of atomic weapon science and technology. Savannah River would produce fuel for H-bombs. One of the greatest civil liberties battles of our times, the Oppenheimer case, grew from the Truman administration's decision to build H-bombs. The controversy swirled around us, and I was avidly attentive. A shameful episode in our history, one for which I can see no shred of justification, is what the government did to ruin J. Robert Oppenheimer. In a signature crusade of the 1950s, small and mean men brought down one of our nation's very best.[2]

My own role at Savannah River was to help steer government money for the habitation, schools, and services required by the thousands of incoming workers. There were about forty thousand at the peak of construction, with new operation workers filtering in every day. Virtually all were white. I suppose I did it well, for pay-raises were regular.

Though Aiken, South Carolina, was a most pleasant place to live, I chose to leave government service to help my wife raise a family and to return to academia. I also had had my fill of the munitions business. I have not again been active with the military. That may, in the opinion of some (including myself for years), disqualify me from writing about it.

If not in the ranks, however, the military and I have had a lot to do with each other. But is this not true with every American of our time? The military has, it seems to me, outlined and provided much content for all of our days, whether we serve in the ranks or simply go our way in civilian life. Since 1945, we have all in one way or another been shaped by the military. In the South it is expected that when strangers first meet to inquire "where you from," and non-Southerners probably get to the same question soon enough. If the meeting continues just a short time it is bound for each to establish where she or he was during the War, or the Korean war, or Vietnam, or what she or he thinks about those wars the two Presidents Bush had us fight in Iraq, or the campaign of President Obama to undertake his chosen war in Afghanistan. The wars of our country are our life markers.

Military actions require, beyond the generals and admirals, troops of

various kinds. Where does the state get them? In many ways, from offer-
ing a share in the booty, as in the days when war was an entrepreneurial
strategy, to inspiring men to join religious crusades. In the United States,
where we have created such monstrous social inequality that the top five
bank executives are paid, as I write this, between $17 million and $23
million each annually, one might think it would be hard to call on our
citizens for military service. Nevertheless, like other modern democracies,
we fill the ranks in large part by appeals to patriotism.

The United States doggedly stays its course of pursuing its goals
through military action or the threat of it. Congress and indeed public
opinion seem convinced that such is our national mission and right. War
is somehow woven into "our way of life." Sadly, tragically, America has
become not the world's indispensable nation, as was once claimed, but
a bulking power that menaces the rationality of international relations.

A well-nigh universal belief is that war may be efficacious if skillfully
managed. But in fact, it seems, wars can never be successfully managed.
That to some minds might be a defense of war; e.g. the Lincoln administration launched the Civil War to crush Southern rebellion, but after
huge deaths and destruction the mission transformed itself into the
overthrow of slavery which otherwise might have long continued. So it
redeemed itself? I don't think so, and neither do many more-qualified
students of history than I. Would slavery's future would have been long
lasting without the war? Who knows?

We hedge our bets on the outcomes of war by speaking of good and
bad wars. The bad ones come to be viewed as somehow unintended, sort
of like reckless driving. So we get judgments like these: Iraq War I—
good; Iraq War II—bad; World War I—bad; and World War II—good.
We contend that the "good" ones are self-justifying and somehow they
excuse the others.

Such is the romance we have imbibed. For most of us in the U.S. the
"bad" wars are simply accepted in the comforting conviction that after all
the "better" side won. Our addiction to war has survived. Texas, California,
New Mexico, and Arizona have rejoiced in the fruits of a particular war
of conquest, which we named the "Mexican War," however iniquitous

it may have been. Puerto Rico, Guam, the Philippines for a while, and Cuba for a shorter while were trophies of our decisive burst into being a "world power" as a result of the Spanish-American War. The applause for the Spanish-American War, except from our native imperialists, is not so great. All nationalists, on the other hand, blessed the Indian wars: they were our manifest destiny.

Wars of conquest have at least such satisfactions. Imperialists, of whom there are still a multitude, rejoiced in them. It was the American practice to win all of our wars, which for many citizens transformed them all into good and just fights. This erased from our active historical memory the strong opposition each war had had when it began. Lately, Americans have not been clearly winning: Vietnam, Iraq, Afghanistan, tomorrow perhaps Iran or Pakistan. Who can know if and when "victory" was or will be achieved? Those wars are in "a fog of ambiguity," as Eugene Robinson, the *Washington Post* commentator, has phrased it. He has gone on to ask, "Who believes the Middle East is a safer place than before the U.S. invasion?"

These presidential wars are immensely expensive and net us little or nothing in return. They seem, in fact, to drag down our economy, unless they have been the essential protector of the oil supplies we feel that without which we cannot live well. These wars have beneficially accelerated the development of all sorts of technologies and cures, but we hardly undertook them with that in mind.

In these twentieth-century wars, we do not conquer new territories as we hugely did during the preceding century. We don't free slaves. We don't hold fast to President Wilson's "Fourteen Points" or President Roosevelt's "Four Freedoms." It can be said that we were indispensable in the overthrow of Nazism and the containment of Communism and that we led in the creation of the United Nations. Those were great achievements. But that seems now too distant to atone for all of our later and arguably aggressive warring.

Militarism willingly accepts no bridle. The War Powers Resolution was passed in 1973 over President Nixon's veto by a Congress feeling the public's outrage over the war in Vietnam, with our 58,261 dead and the hundreds of thousands our allies and enemies lost. Congress wanted to put a repeat of that war-making out of easy presidential reach. The old Kellogg-Briand Treaty of the 1920s had made its try; here now was another. That older effort wanted to outlaw war; the War Powers Resolution would merely tame it a bit. The operative provision, however, was quite specific:

> The constitutional powers of the President as Commander-in-Chief to introduce United States Armed Forces into hostilities . . . are exercised only pursuant to (1) a declaration of war, (2) specific statutory authorization, or (3) a national emergency created by an attack upon the United States, its territories or possessions, or its armed forces.

Every president since Nixon, Democratic or Republican, has wriggled his way under and around compliance with it. President Obama did, too, and he may have come closer than any predecessor to flat-out violation.

Militarism has become the nation's dominating policy. It rules to the point where military power has, in fact, become Americanism in the view of millions of people beyond our borders and a sadly large number within them.[3]

4

TIME AND PLACE

Greenbrier County, West Virginia, is where I first came from. It is a remarkably lovely place on its eastern side. I never travel Highway 219 between Lewisburg and Marlinton, in peaceful Pocahontas County, without reveling at the simple beauty of the approach from the north into Renick, or the byway of the Brownstown one-lane road out of Renick circling back to 219, or the quiet warmth of the road from Frankford to Maxwelton, and beyond on fearsome twists and turns to Williamsburg. I marvel that persons would have wanted to live, and still do, in their well-kept small village at this quiet, hidden intersection of two mountain roads, seemingly coming from and going to nowhere.

The intersecting road from the west will bring a traveler to the site of the Battle of Fort Donnally where in 1778 the colonials fought and defeated the Shawnee and their chieftain, Cornstalk. Nearby is also the site of the last recorded lynching in the state, in 1932. After the road's eventual connection with Route 60, it will lead you in not many miles to the coal mines. They are small in comparison to the huge ones, mountains strip-mined and topped in villainous destruction, in the neighboring counties to the west. Arrogant devastation.

Turn now and go back to Lewisburg and watch out for an inconspicuous sign pointing the way to the well-shaded Civil War cemetery. What you will find is a mass grave for more than a hundred unknown Confederate soldiers, losers in the battle of Lewisburg of May 2, 1863. The battle was short in duration and lowly rated by historians, but it reportedly took the lives of ninety-five Confederate soldiers and gave grievous wounds to many more. One estimate of Union deaths I have seen is thirteen. West Virginians were divided in their sympathies and loyalties; this Lewisburg corner of the county and state was Confederate.

The bodies of their dead soldiers were left behind, stacked on the street, it is said, until the Yankees got out of town. Then they were buried in this common grave which was dug in the shape of a cross.

Find your way for a short distance to the Old Stone Church which was built in 1796 by early settlers who had crossed into these Allegheny Mountains with their modest utilitarian possessions and had somehow a remarkable vision in their minds, of a simple unadorned stone church of rigorously clean lines, which they wanted to build. It is still in use. Nearby is the monument to the Confederacy, which for some reason was moved in the recent past from a more prominent location. Read now the inscription carved above the church's entrance in rough lettering:

THIS

BUILDING WAS

ERRECTED IN THE YEAR

1796 AT THE EXPENCE

OF A FEW OF THE FIRST

INHABITANTS OF THIS

LAND TO COMMEMORATE

THEIR AFFECTION &

ESTEEM FOR THE

HOLY GOSPEL OF

JESUS CHRIST

READER

IF YOU ARE INCLINED

TO APPLAUD THEIR

VIRTUES GIVE GOD

THE GLORY

Cross the street to a historical marker remembering the life of Dick Pointer. He was a slave, credited with outstanding bravery at the Battle of Fort Donnally. Mr. Pointer applied to the state of Virginia (which this area belonged to until June 20, 1863, when West Virginia was created) for a warrior's pension, but he was denied. He was finally freed in 1807 and died in 1827. From his story I am fairly sure one could make rich commentary about war, slavery, and justice, a story that would be true and differing little from hundreds or more similar true stories.

But I wonder what need there is for further moralizing or even philosophizing about the cruelty of racism or, indeed, of the injustice of society. That has been done to near-perfection by a long line of humanity's best minds. We can, of course, pile on examples and reflections, and that is, I think, socially valuable. We may be, after all, better people than many of our forerunners—such as the classical and much-honored Athenians who vented their savagery on conquered foes, as in massacring all the men of the defeated island of Melos and annihilating the island itself.

Slavery and annihilation—we have to rid ourselves of the past. But not all of it. Big pieces of it are needed for moving ahead, or else like the western Europeans in post-Roman years we might stagger and stumble about for a few centuries of self-discovery. The experiences of this small Appalachian "land" are a good place to start one's self-discovery. I stand in awe of the ancestors who pioneered here and then left the land better than they found it; who built this lovely church structure and built it to last; who would dig such a hallowed grave for burying their dead; who included a brave man determined to be a free man and others who would persevere in support of him. But I also see in the story a society taking land from a weaker society and then turning to making war with each other.

Americans are a great people, with great faults. We are a menacing people. We are also the people who took in many of Europe's poorest, and Asia's too, and granted them a harsh homeplace where they could as they would make a better life for themselves. We also took in Africa's poorest, though first we enslaved them. We are the people who even before we became "a people" wrote for ourselves and accepted a Constitution which with lots of imperfections was nevertheless something new and wonderful under the sun, our birth certificate as it were, our assertion of a special place among the nations of the world even though we did not have gaudy birthrights.

We, in fact, had hardly more than this piece of paper we had written ourselves. We are the people who unjustly grabbed our land from its native inhabitants and have had a tortured conscience ever since, which is another of our peculiarities because most conquerors in other times and places had neither regrets nor remorse. But we did, and stumblingly now seek our conquereds' participation in our nation making.

The thing I like about that dedicatory statement carved at the front of the Old Stone Church is that it contains not a word, not a syllable, of praise of the national state. It is all about religion, citizens, and self-reliance and believers. Perhaps that was because in 1796 these folks had not yet got used to being American "patriots," or for some weightier reason did not want to mix their allegiances. Whatever the reason, they were avoiding the treacherous fault line of being a patriotic church that snares religion, before and in our days.

5

The Church

Why We Keep It Separate

To evade the snare of being the ruler's church had once been the great achievement of strong elements of Protestant Christianity. Before the Reformation and since the time of the emperor Constantine, church and empire shaped Europe's culture, and politics too, by a sort of negotiation, a peace between powers of equal rights and assumed Christian duties. The achievement was the avoidance of turning this new faith into a civil religion, merging God and the flags of the several nations emerging from what had been their medieval and Renaissance status. State and Ecclesia had shared religion and powers in the Christian world, and most emphatically still do, though the religions most to be feared are the civil ones that deify state powers. The danger was never more present than today as some so-called evangelical denominations seek their power by tying themselves to every bit of Americanism that lures them and as Roman Catholics aggressively seek to set rules and practices for private behavior.

For professing Christians, it might seem that a first question they must ask of themselves is: should I not be a Mennonite (or one of similar sects), living peacefully apart from the state and from the seeking of riches, in emulation of Jesus and the little band of beggars he gathered to himself? For myself, I answer "no" and so have most believers through the centuries; but at least in the history of Christianity there has always been the fundamental belief, at some degree of intensity, that religion has its own duties, separate from those of the state.

How did the "separation of church and state" come about? We can say that it began with the words of Jesus to the Pharisees when they asked whether his teaching allowed paying taxes to the Roman power. He replied, "render to Caesar the things which are Caesar's and unto God the things that are God's." It has been difficult ever since to decide what are the things of the state and what are not, but the important fact is that dualism: the insistence that beside state power, which is to be obeyed, there is an unearthly power, also to be obeyed in some mode. This unearthly power stands independent of the state power, and it is not imaginary but is in fact God being active in human affairs.[4]

The political theorizing of the West after Rome has developed in the context that church and state are separate. Not before the Renaissance and great figures such as Machiavelli in the sixteenth century did political thought venture far outside that context, did not adhere to the conviction that truth had its boundaries and that those limits had been provided to men by the Scriptures. It would take another couple of centuries before thinkers would acknowledge that they were free of those boundaries and that in modern times we live in a basically secular civilization.

But the past clings and has its rights, and we speak of and believe in the rights of conscience, and even the dictates of conscience, and have given some legal and institutional form to them. In the United States we have our written Constitution whose first principle is that it itself is enforceable law, and it is within that protection that the American principle of church-state separation has developed. The First Amendment says that Congress shall make no law respecting an establishment of religion or prohibiting the free exercise thereof. This has been enlarged by extensive interpretation to mean not only Congress but also the state governments and, in fact, any type of governmental action.

Constitutional law speaks of two clauses in the Amendment: the establishment clause and the free exercise clause. "Separation of church and state" has had to be inferred because those words are not in the text, and not clearly or consistently in the practice in the early days of the Republic. The two clauses are, I think, closely related and either stands well enough alone: free exercise would not exist if a particular church is "established."

The fact that the Constitution does not use the words leads now and then to denial by some evangelicals of the constitutionality of required "separation." Their desire is that government acknowledge this to be a Christian nation. Political wisdom has fortunately dissented.

The concepts protected by the First Amendment have been entrusted to law and lawyers, a result of the principle of enforceability of the provisions of our written Constitution. In our country with its mixture of faiths and their adherents, this is, I think, probably good. The constitutional law that has resulted contains some silliness, as judges and lawyers try to make life conform to their ways of speaking. We thus have a plethora of distinctions without much difference on laboriously litigated issues, dealing with trivia, by believers who take them seriously or by non-believers who are ardently annoyed by them. Matters like, for example, where on public property can statuary depicting the Ten Commandments be placed; or the wording of the Pledge of Allegiance (okay or not okay for children in a classroom to say "under God "?); and such. The latest I have seen is whether little boys should be circumcised. Voters in California may have to vote on this.

The puzzling legal conceptualizing of church-state separation is made all the more so when it has to be done within the richly varied and always changing ways people practice their worship. Styles change in worship as elsewhere though the faiths do not. I think the state should be careful to let them, like other fluids, find their own level.

The African American Christian congregations—both Catholic and Protestant—do not have all the same minor beliefs and practices as do the "white" congregations. This is conspicuously so concerning separation of church and state. Direct and prominent involvement in electoral politics is customary for them and their ministers. None, not even the ACLU, seems to mind, yet.

Islamic congregations have strong views about the political issues in Arab and other Moslem countries. Jewish congregations tend to choose sides on the political debates and elections that go on within Israel and to have strong opinions about how Washington should treat Israel, and they freely involve themselves in those debates. The rest of us should stand down, nearly always, I think.

Ours is the republic of a nation that for good or for ill includes members (adherents may be a better term) of many organized religious bodies. I think this fact is one of our greatest national strengths and virtues. Tolerance is a social necessity and has to be practiced to maintain civil peace.

Americans are by overwhelming majorities committed to tolerance and accept that having and practicing a religion is a precious right. Little law is needed in support of what is our predisposed value. We should congratulate ourselves because religion can also be a great divider when it seeks to enforce its precepts through the power of the state, which, for example, becomes a serious problem when the church calls on the state to enforce its rules of sexuality.

Christianity was born apart from any "state." There is much mythologizing about those origins, but whether fact or myth little bothers most of us, and that is true of how the Old Testament is accepted by Christians or, in my observation, how the Torah and the rest of the Hebrew Bible are accepted by Reformed and Conservative Jews. Orthodox Christians have historically had closer ties to their "states." Judaism and Christianity have, for at least the millennia of European and both North and South American civil societies, inherently held that civil and religious obedience are different loyalties. This has meant that political theory and discourse were, for centuries, carried on within the framework of those dominating social institutions and from them habits of thought and inherited values sprang.

One gets the impression that too many current preachers would de-intellectualize faith, and that retrogression often prevails. Perhaps they will succeed; they are one unfortunate expression of the current secular gospel of change.

There is an old Protestant hymn which those of us who grew up in one of its evangelical denominations can probably remember singing, with our usual small regard for the words. That is all the more probable because the rolling marching rhythm of this hymn overrides words; when the congregation gets into it you can almost hear the drums roll.

We've a story to tell to the nations,
That shall turn their hearts to the right.
A story of truth and mercy,
A story of peace and light,
A story of peace and light.

We've a song to be sung to the nations,
That shall lift their hearts to the Lord,
A song that shall conquer evil
And shatter the spear and sword,
And shatter the spear and sword.

For the darkness shall turn to dawning,
And the dawning to noonday bright;
And Christ's great kingdom shall come on earth,
The kingdom of love and light.

Who are the "we" who would boldly and self-confidently, almost glee-fully, sing such a song, and what are we believing while we sing it? That it could really be? This is religious optimism at its best. I would say that the antithetical hymn and unfortunately one just as true to Protestantism is "Onward Christian Soldiers," dogmatic and militarist.

I am a Baptist, a Roger Williams Baptist, and my denomination grew from the Anabaptists of the fifteenth and sixteenth centuries who stoutly resisted the state and wars (though by the next century they had become Baptists and no longer much resisted either). Ancient values, however, continue to haunt all Christianity. And so some of us worry about the morality of war. Some theologians have resolved those worries in the same way St. Augustine did and have decided that "political right" cannot always be the "moral right" and that, as Reinhold Niebuhr once famously taught, moral man must find a home within immoral society. St. Augustine had taught that the "good believer lives firstly" as a citizen of a heavenly city, not his earthly one (so too teaches much of the He-brew and Christian Bibles; so too had Plato), and this other-worldliness is an enduring trait within the creeds and occasionally an active one. Modernity is uncomfortable with it; I think rightly so.

I would like to suggest (with acknowledgment to former Defense Secretary Weinberger) one more rule for assessing the legitimacy of any war: does it have well-understood purposes, approved by public opinion, and are they likely to be achieved? It seems to me that to send human beings to kill or to be killed (as is still being done in Afghanistan) and to destroy homes and social order is immoral in "lost causes." War is too serious for revenge, or romance, or adventure, or blundering.

Pickett's Charge was an immoral action because it was foolhardy. So I think that moral people in and out of houses of worship should be questioning the likelihood of realizing the purposes of this current war our nation is fighting: a war against an "ism"—terrorism. Such a war, served by bombing and otherwise carrying destruction to a far away land and people, should be questioned on the fundamental grounds of whether it is winnable. What thoughtful person can really believe that we will lick terrorism? Maybe kill a few leaders, even push them off stage, but we will not "win." In the end, terrorists will always remain.

But if we do indeed reduce the terrorists, where next will we choose to direct the enormous war-making machine we have built with our genius, treasure, sweat, and many lives?

We've a story to tell to the nations. What is the actual truth in it? In this ecumenical age a phrase has become widely used: people of faith. What is different about them from many others who do not profess a faith?

I think that people of faith—Muslims, Jews, Christians—must be protective of life and thus must make a personal decision about when the taking of another's life—of a prisoner, a fetus, a civilian in time of war, a soldier—is morally acceptable. But people who do not subscribe to a religious faith could do likewise. What is different about religious folks?

The difference can be that in addition to our moral judgment, religious persons are under orders.

I won't presume to speak of the commands of other faiths, but as a Baptist I do not discover any command within Christianity which directs one to put the interests of the state—put what might be called patriotism—above that which the hymnist calls the "kingdom of love and light."

I cannot discover any command within New Testament Christianity to exact an eye for an eye and therefore I do not support wars for revenge.

Nor can I discover within Christianity where any of us, not even our president, has been appointed to be judge of what is "evil." Instead what I do believe is that none of us has authority to be such a judge. To claim that power is almost blasphemy.

In arguing political or military policies, churches will probably lose every contest in which they are foolish enough to engage. The proper and also essential role of the moral person seems to me to be to question strongly the state whenever it trumps our moral judgment by claiming national security. The further essential role of the Christian church, synagogues, and mosques, too, is to assert to the state, "Your ends, your agenda, are not necessarily ours."

6

The South

The Testing of Democracy

The South is a well-liked habitation for many persons, myself included. We tend to be ones who have for long, even ancestrally, lived here. Its appeal, however, is felt by many others as well. There is an oft-heard remark, attributed to an eminent scholar, that Southerners are good people who do bad things, despite their better natures, where race is concerned. This self-appraisal could be objected to on several grounds, the chief being variations on the old adage that actions speak more clearly than words. In my own observation, white Southerners are as morally good as folks anywhere, but the political leaders they choose, which tends to mean choose to follow, have throughout American history been abysmally bad. The South's political leaders have been a heavy burden for all of American democracy and still are.

Worst of all, of course, were the ones who led the nation into the Civil War and who have ever since been honored, even venerated, for doing so.

Similar admiration has been granted to the so-called Redeemers of post-Civil War times who restored the Democratic Party and ousted blacks from any political role: men such as Cole Blease and Ben Tillman of South Carolina and Tom Watson and Henry Grady of Georgia and, in later years, Carter Glass of Virginia (a favorite of my father), Richard Russell of Georgia, and John Stennis of Mississippi. There were also more unpleasant fellows, and plenty of them—the likes of the Talmadges, Lester Maddox, Theodore Bilbo, "Cotton Ed" Smith, et al.

Such political leaders—and indeed they did lead—achieved what the Civil War heroes did not or could not do. They successfully accomplished just about all that the Secessionists had essentially sought. They wrested any shred of power from Negro Southerners and firmly, it was thought, secured white supremacy throughout the region, impoverishing the South as they did so. And pretty much, as by the 1890s would become evident, the South's white political leaders got the rest of the nation to accept this and even applaud. Nor is this development surprising. In this region, which war-making had made penurious, the black Southerners were poorest of all in wealth and education and remained so until their own historic efforts, and the migration of many thousands to the north and west, lifted up their painful progress.

And if by our day, the South's political leadership has cast off its commitment to a segregated society, the second of its historical commitments, to military greatness and power, has been retained and is faithfully honored by the South's representatives in Congress. This too is not surprising, for the culture and the politics of the Southern states had been grounded on the practice or the threat of whatever violence was needed to enforce slavery and segregation, to enforce white supremacy. The most deep-rooted of Southern traditions is acceptance of the ever-readiness of the force needed to maintain its position. The utility of arms has been bred into the Southern culture.

This has carried over into the regional congressional solidarity in support of the Pentagon's interests; also to the trigger-happy demands of the National Rifle Association. Were it not for Southern congressmen and congresswomen, the chances are that our nation would enjoy drastically lower military expenditures and far more effective gun control.

One outgrowth in particular is the vast horde of guns in private ownership, and now beyond meaningful public regulation following the present Supreme Court's 2008 decision in the case of *District of Columbia v. Heller*.[5] The Second Amendment was drafted so poorly that what its words exactly mean is, in fact, unknowable; not even by the gaggle of lawyers who have in recent times chosen to enter what had been, and properly so, a political debate. The National Rifle Association and other advocates of "gun rights" dragged the Amendment from the closet to which an earlier Supreme Court, in *U.S. v. Miller*, had sensibly rested it in 1939.[6] What we have now is a subversion of "domestic tranquility," entangling the Constitution in raucous and unrelenting popular debate.

When the "rights" of gun-owners are championed, by the courts or almost anyone, the messenger is preaching to the already converted. And in the South, Southerners want to be with each other. Internal dissent does not come easy, ever. In W. J. Cash's masterful book, *The Mind of the South*[7], which still reads today with about as much accuracy as when published in 1940, he spoke of this social phenomenon as "solidification" and traced its history to white Southerners' need to define themselves, first of all, as whites. It is amazing, really, that the compulsion to "solidify" survives, despite much in-migration of newcomers. And so it has not been a surprise that the South has moved from being "solid" Democratic to being "solid" Republican. Youths are bringing in some cracks in the solidity but Cash's "savage ideal" is still intact "whereunder dissent and variety are . . . suppressed and men become virtual replicas of one another." I have allowed for change and progress by deleting Cash's own word, "completely," before "suppressed."

In fact nearly the same "solidification," the same centripetal force, still prevails. It has allied itself with the rigid "conservatism" of the modern Republican Party, and it has become more threatening to national democracy than it ever was.

For instance, the Glass Steagall Act of 1933, a law that required banks to keep their investment business separate from their deposit and loan business, was a stabilizing force in banking for generations. It was brought about by a rock-ribbed conservative Southern pair, Senator Carter Glass of Virginia and Representative Henry Bascom Steagall of Alabama. Its repeal in 1999 was also driven by conservative Southerners, two of the three sponsors being Phil Gramm of Texas and Tom Bliley of Virginia, but whereas eighty years ago conservatism meant controlling the excesses of capital so that banks would not drown in risk and so that small banks could survive, in 1999 it meant loosening the restraints on big banks so that they could grow ever larger. The majority of Southern congressmen followed along each time. Many analysts see the banking crisis of 2007 to 2011 as a result of this repeal.

Carter Glass was an interesting figure. Elected first in 1902 to the House of Representatives, he went to the Senate in 1920 and stayed there until his death in 1946. Public finances especially interested him. He is usually credited with being the chief mover not only of Glass-Steagall but also, and probably even more importantly, the creation of the Federal Reserve System in 1913, and he looked after it throughout his tenure. He also seems to have been a deep-dyed racist in every ancestral chord of his being. It is interesting that the Federal Reserve is now attacked by conservatives as government over-reaching into the private financial sphere.

There have been other Southern political leaders like him who, despite their racial attitudes, prominently led in some progressive causes. Senator Fulbright of Arkansas, who wrote the last "learned" argument in favor of segregation that I can remember reading in his amicus brief in the great Supreme Court decision of *Aaron v. Cooper* (it was, happily, rejected by the Court) became a strong voice against the Vietnam War and the parent of the creative program of "Fulbright" scholarships for study abroad. Such persons seem no longer to exist among us, so tightly drawn are the ideological demands of the Republican Party.

But there were always glimmers of doubt as to the rightness of the South's society. I often have thought that the true "redeemers" of the South have nearly all been its women. Legions of them, my mother one of them, insisting that her children not use the vernacular, but say instead "colored people." On such tiny steps civilization is built. And the women of the South took bigger steps than that when increasing numbers let their husbands know that they did not need lynching to protect their virtue.

The only grandparent I ever knew was my maternal grandmother, and not for long; she died at ninety-three when I was nine. She had been a teen when General Phil Sheridan and his troops swept through the Shenandoah Valley destroying all they could. I have one of those hazy childhood memories of hearing her say that her family had to "live in the woods" in his wake.

That grandfather was a Southern Methodist minister and, as was the Methodist practice, moved about a lot, in Virginia and West Virginia. His name was Joseph Crickenberger, and he was a descendant of the German settlers of the Staunton–Harrisonburg area. The family name then was possibly Krikenberger. Some say these settlers are descendants of the Hessian soldiers who had been British mercenaries in the Revolutionary War. Could be. How my Scot stock and my German stock got together I do not know. Ours is another example of historical variety within Southern character. The Methodists who had split into South and North before the Civil War got back together again, though not until 1940. The Presbyterians did a few years later. The Baptists haven't yet. Late in my career I was a board member of a small peace-minded foundation, and we gave our largest grant to another noble seed of those German settlers, the Eastern Mennonite University, located in Harrisonburg.

There was in the South, however, always uneasy doubt as to whether they were right about the morality of their racial practices. I was once jolted into awareness of that doubting. (Is there a more honorable word in our language than "doubt"? It's what we human beings, at our best, do. It rates with "love" and "justice" as openers of the doors to civilization.)

My jolt came when my seventh grade teacher assigned us to the reading of a biography. Our choice of subject was to be presented to the class as a candidate for the classroom's "hall of fame." The criterion was to be, "Having made by his life's work the world a better place."

I selected Stonewall Jackson, great warrior, great Presbyterian, great Christian. In my turn I proudly nominated him and was then incredulous when Ms. Arnold responded—before the whole class!—by saying that she could not see that my man had much made the world better by his warring. This she said in P.S. 49, the Robert E. Lee Junior High School! She said it to me, a recent graduate of Baltimore's P.S. 14, the Sydney Lanier Elementary School, named for the South's finest poet! Experiences like that are the good luck some of us have had, and better it is to have them when young.

I have not read another biography of General Jackson since nor, for that matter that of any other General—not my cup of tea. I am, nevertheless, willing to believe that the usual military leader is a good person even as in my judgment he is professionally engaged in doing bad things, very bad ones; and whether he be Lee, MacArthur, Eisenhower, Nimitz, or Petraeus, this is true whether or not his neighbors and fellow church members admire him. A man's or woman's good standing among other women and men does not justify his or her acceptance of slavery—or war-making.

The first task of the civil rights movement was to require the non-South to stop "making nice " with the South, to stop allowing JFK—it was too late to stop FDR—from constantly finding a more important political action (often involving foreign policy) that needed Southern Congressmen's backing; and thus the African Americans' cause would have to wait. This had been the wall that Representative Adam Clayton Powell had struggled to climb, before our country was reshaped, almost reinvented, by the great legislation enacted under President Lyndon Johnson's leadership, the Civil Rights Act of 1964 and the Voting Rights Act of 1965.

In 1962 I was invited by the Tuskegee Institute to give the Commencement Address for its summer session graduates. It happens that in 1962 I had driven the length of U.S. 29 from the vicinity of Pensacola, Florida, to Washington, D.C., and although I had driven from north to south it was easy enough to imagine doing the reverse. My trip was before the era of Interstates, and the imagery which absorbed me was how full of modern American history it was; U.S. 29 was loaded with places where great events had occurred. So I decided to tell about that in my speech.

Pensacola was to have its initial school desegregation that coming fall, and we watched nervously in those years to see how the successive "first times" of those historic developments would turn out. The towns I went through were like battlefronts: Atlanta, Charlotte, Greensboro, and Farmville, Virginia, which shut down its public schools for about four years in defiance of national law.

Tuskegee in August, with little or no air conditioning, is an intimidating prospect. With the heavy black robes the graduates and I wore, one could only sweat through it. The theme of my talk was that all of the South's deepest problems were being carried from the towns as along U.S. 29 to Washington for resolution. The period of the South's guardianship under the authority of Washington had begun.

I won't carry this experience further except to remember that as I drove I kept thinking in a driver's solitude that the years of "mingled meanness and greatness of soul" that the South of the 1960s was going through must be having a lasting effect on its youth. I have had the same worried questions about the effects on the young of the constant wars and all of the other raw and brutalizing events since.

So I wonder, will there ever be peace in our world as long as there are generals, captains, and midshipmen in line to make their combat marks and to win the honors those marks bring? My answer is, no. And measured by Ms. Arnold's criterion, what civilizing work did they all do? How did they make life any better?

And I wonder, too, as a citizen of this uniquely "indispensable" democracy, whether we will continue to embrace the "big tent" or whether like the Czechs and Slovaks we will find that the union is not worth the effort. But if we forsake our calling of being the "big tent," what would our national life then become?

7

TIMOCRATS AND OLIGARCHS

Plato spoke of a form of government he called "timocracy." Such a government as he defined it would be led by tested and proven warriors, men (or possibly women) dedicated through a strong sense of honor and by respect for learning and art to fulfilling their duties. They would have been freed from material wants and concerns—including child-rearing—by a wise ordering of classes.

Nevertheless, Plato reasoned, bad tendencies would inevitably spring up even in his idealized state and would press the government to slacken the bonds of honor and trend toward a perversion of itself; in short toward oligarchy. Wealth thus would supplant honor as the state's organizing principle.[8] Aristotle followed Plato, using the same word briefly, but timocracy for him meant simply oligarchy.

It seems to me that there is a more complete thought when both nouns are used and their dual meanings preserved. Timocracy and oligarchy form, I think, the two forces that are the principal definition of the ruling class or, if preferred, the governing class of nearly all modern states, modern democracies in particular.

But if the military does not openly or directly rule, it is nevertheless generally seen as indispensable in ways that no other class or occupation is. A state could exist for a while without teachers, preachers, lawyers, farmers, or merchants, but it is hardly conceivable that one could do without a military, at least not in the midst of other states.

In modern governments as well as pre-democratic ones the military is, if not the indispensable class, close to being so. Generally even its lower officer ranks will go through their lives held in high esteem. As often as not, the honors that military leaders receive may be well-deserved, especially when contrasted with the records of the generality of others who achieve high ranks in our government and business affairs. Often talented persons are recruited from the military to handle important diplomatic and other governmental missions, and generally seem to do well.

And especially at the very highest levels, civilian leaders in modern governments intermingle with military officers in what becomes a circulating elite of the governing class. The timocrats and the oligarchs unite into a political nexus of decision-makers, where they intermingle with those who have risen from other directions, not gaining their distinction from either wealth or military honor but from industry, university administration, or scholarship. But very seldom, at least in the United States, from trade union leadership. The governing class expands, in pace with the expansion of government and its military and related occupations.

America's spreading economic involvements abroad have caused it to divide the world into regions, or "commands," each directed by a military officer of flag rank. The United States "African command" has recently been in the news, although, as far as anyone knows, we have no military engagement except in the Arab states of North Africa. But it is another "command." I do not know the usual extent of their powers but the appointees do act as overseers of our interests and expand yet further the cadre of elite leaders. If America's influence abroad were to decline, this would change. In fact, that decline has seemingly already begun as decisions and policies are formed by or within other nations which in a recent past would have waited for a greenlight from us.

Why do we have such officials? The role and power of the federal government have perhaps been the most durable political issue in American history since our independence. The Constitution's preamble would seem the right guide to the leaders needed and their responsibilities. None of the noble purposes stated there includes the managing of the affairs of other nations or peoples.

Several, perhaps lesser, developments are outcomes of the expanded functions of the military. The military's role as the indispensable class results also from its wide-ranging functions.

Parallel to the argument that some businesses have become too big to be allowed by the government to fail, the military likewise can hardly ever be reduced. The consequences of any substantial retrenchment might be devastating to the country's economic welfare. It has apparently become unthinkable and unspeakable for a president or a Congress to propose reducing "defense." What could be done with all the surplus materiel, personnel, assembly lines and funds, here and at bases throughout the world? President Obama and the Congress serving with him have made a tentative effort to do so; if it is sustained, it may bring timocracy down a bit. But neither political party ventures to advocate appreciable reductions in "defense" even though its present size far exceeds that of other nations. We dominate the planet though time and again other and apparently weaker peoples turn back our imposing strength, which might be a sign of bad generals, or bad causes, or both.

The permanence of the military class encourages the implantation of military culture throughout the larger society as more persons "serve" and as political policies become offshoots of military ones and vice-versa.

The United States' populace seems, to this citizen, to be unable to give up addictions to drugs, and that causes us to send our police into Mexico and our soldiers to invade Afghanistan seeking to control, in Mexico especially, the vicious violence produced by gangsters assaulting each other over shares in the profits made by supplying our citizens with illegal substances. This death-dealing could probably be ended, or at least greatly reduced, if our Congress would decriminalize these drugs so that they would cease being a lush territory for gangsters. Instead of doing that we build, at enormous expense and spawning the hate of our southern neighbors, a fence—a fence intended to protect us in some way from those neighbors whom we would wall off as being an inferior people.

Because of our enormous cultural and military investment, this war on drugs, like all our ongoing wars, won't end because it can't. We have laced warring into our American political natures as the policy to which we instinctively turn for dealing with our most troublesome problems. As the Afghanistan and Iraqi wars slow, we hear, from many sides of our political parties and factions, voices saying that we must keep a "presence" there, that the region is too unsteady to be left to manage itself, that we, after all, have "responsibilities." After that some newer region, say Australia, may need our presence.

The militarization of our politics cannot but yield a weakening of the constraints of the Constitution, especially those of the Bill of Rights and the other rights guaranteed by the Constitution such as habeas corpus. At least equally important is the damaging effect it will almost certainly have on the structural plan of our government, i.e., the separation of powers and federalism. As important as that is the danger that the military spirit, encouraged strongly, can squeeze the live spirit from our other cultural elements.

The dominating presence in our governing bodies of any single social or economic class, whether military, economic, or religious (or Ivy League graduates), has to be noted and feared. The military has far greater potential for republican overthrow, even peaceful, than has any other class. There are contemporary nation-states where rule requires the consent of its military, which is their version of "consent of the governed." Its arrival here is not unthinkable.

This process of the almost organic spread and toughening of the military presence in our society has become evident to many observers and, indeed, to the many thousands who in their daily lives adapt themselves to it. It has become strikingly more pronounced as the republic has abandoned any form of obligatory military service in favor of all-volunteer forces, creating a separate estate as it were.

Plato's timocracy devolves into oligarchy. Aristotle's begins and ends there. What seems to be the case in modern democracies, such as the United States, is that the power of wealth and the power of arms have merged and do jointly lead our ruling class. The easiest of predictions is that this will continue to be the case. Oligarchy is, as Robert Michels tells us in the next chapter, the fate darkening the future of all democracies, including ours. Almost as certain a prediction is that this may be a lasting condition.

8

Nation Building

A ruling class is the norm in all political societies, though not always happily acknowledged. The composition of the class varies with time and place and other circumstances. Robert Michel's 1915 book, *Political Parties*, is a classic of political science and is one of the seminal studies of the class in modern democracies.

Michels was bold enough to announce his conclusion that there is an "iron law of oligarchy" in democracies. "Social wealth cannot be satisfactorily administered in any other manner than by the creation of an extensive bureaucracy. In this way we are led by an inevitable logic to the flat denial of the possibility of a state without classes."[9]

Many have dissented from this not very likeable holding—scholars of several persuasions and contemporary Tea Party folks among them—but not with notable success. The protests known as the Occupy Wall Street movement focused on the growing disparity of wealth and income especially in the largest and richest national economies. Their virtually spontaneous actions targeted financial capitalism in the wake of a severe recession they believed—reasonably—to have been caused by reckless and frequently dishonest investing by banks. Whether or not their movement, without clear goals and leaders by design, will have lasting impact, the quarrel will nevertheless not go away because there are classes in America.[10]

We do have a ruling class or, if preferred, a governing class. As I have said, I like Plato's suggestion that at least in theory the military class has its own existence alongside the oligarchy. It does not seem in my observation to be necessarily succeeded and replaced by the oligarchs. The lesson of world history is that the military can go its own way. There are states where the army leads pretty much on its own, or as in Zimbabwe where organized thugs lead. But in modern democracies as in the United States we have a dual ruling class, the military and the rich each supportive of the other. And in the future the likely development is merger: the military and the oligarchs merge into the class which supplies rule or governance. Our Constitution's framers wisely tried to steer away from this ever happening, but without success.

It is important to keep always in mind that democracy can mean many things to many different people. It is a very big tent indeed. To me, democracy means that kind of society where public opinion generally prevails without recourse to force. A democratic society is always a country in struggle with itself. And it determines its own ruling class. Popular sovereignty, an old term in USA history, was a good defining term for democracy. Harold Lasswell was, it seems to me, largely correct in saying that the subject of politics and therefore of political science is, at bottom, who gets what, when, and how. If clothed too with its other ideals (in addition to popular sovereignty)—ones which I think have to be earned in political struggle and are more attainable in a democratic system then in any other government or society—we have liberal democracy. That includes:

—the rule of law;

—and protection of individual liberties from the government;

—and from overbearing economic elites.

Our times have been the stage for strong actions by people seeking to change their governments or their constitutions. We call these acts "movements," and we indeed have had a lot of them. As I write these pages the Mideast is literally aflame with the movements that are changing it, probably forever.

Only some movements succeed but, weak or strong, the disturbances they cause are often long-lasting. People of all kinds are constant stirrers of the social pot. Some political movements of our times have been hideous in their natures and outcomes. The worst (so far) were the totalitarian regimes that ruled much of Europe and Asia prior to World War II. It seems to us today almost unbelievable that this could have happened in societies like Germany, Italy, Russia, and Spain with their marvelous histories. But it did.

It is also worth remembering that it was while Americans of an earlier but not far distant day were still fellow members of the same British polity with such great persons as Shakespeare, Milton, Locke, Newton, Burke, Hume—the names are like a roll of honor—that human slavery existed and was not widely questioned, even by these humanitarians. Hard also to accept that slavery lasted for centuries without a lot of objection from these sort of greats and that its successor in the land of Washington, Jefferson, and Madison would be the regime of white supremacy, which was nearly as loathsome. We sometimes must ask ourselves whether the cruel upending of life that once occurred in the richly civilized cultures of Europe, and particularly in those storied civil societies of Germany, Spain, and Italy, could happen here or in our other Atlantic neighbors. I believe it could. We have, after all, come close.

I think the historic menace of our South is huge, since historically the South has been resolutely determined to shape our whole nation. And how would it shape this special nation which has embodied the hopes of so many throughout the world but is now overweight in its power and is therefore a potential troublemaker for every other nation? Into a replica of the South's own oligarchic culture? One of the South's recent unasked-for gifts to the rest of the nation is the Tea Party.

The Tea Partiers are, of course, far from being all of one kind. Some carry the banner of the "know nothing" types who have been a constant presence in American history; some are descendants of the red-baiters of modern times, also a constant of our history; some are worried by the social change going on faster than they can be comfortable with; some are Republican Party leaders opportunistically recruiting for the GOP. Some are also thoughtful citizens, whose essential concern and belief is that government has grown too big.

My belief, however, is that the root of all this serious fault-finding is not what the Tea Partiers or Southern stump preachers think it is. My view is that in American society there is too much money, and much too much of it is in too few hands.

Where, for instance, does all the PAC money come from? One, like myself, can be frightened by the sums thrown into our elections and the probable ways the throwers are paid back. A great deal of it seems to originate or pass through the hands of persons I have hardly heard of: the USA breeds fortunes promiscuously.

There is nothing particularly new or novel about this proposition that the concentration of wealth is dangerous. Conservatives themselves have, over the centuries, flagged it. Aristotle was aware of this ancient money problem and wrote a lot about it. He said:

> It . . . is the greatest happiness which the citizens [of a democracy] can enjoy to possess a moderate and convenient fortune; for when some possess too much, and others nothing at all, the government must either be in the hands of the meanest rabble or else a pure oligarchy; or, from the excesses of both, a tyranny; for this arises from a headstrong democracy or an oligarchy; but very seldom when the members of the community are nearly on an equality with each other.[11]

Aristotle's great and most influential admirer was St. Thomas Aquinas, who spoke likewise:

> Now man is a natural unit, but the unity of a community, which is peace, must be brought into being by the skill of the ruler. To ensure the well-being of a community, therefore, three things are necessary. In the first place the community must be united in peaceful unity. In the second place, the community, thus united, must be directed towards well-doing. For just as a man could do no good if he were not an integral whole, so also a community of men which is disunited and at strife within itself, is hampered in well-doing. Thirdly and finally, it is necessary that there be, through the ruler's sagacity, a sufficiency of those material goods which are indispensable to well-being . . . For since every man is part of the community, all that any man is or has, is in reference to the community.[12]

And of course there was Adam Smith, a main pillar of capitalism:

Is this improvement in the circumstances of the lower ranks of the people to be regarded as an advantage or as an inconveniency to the society? [Smith had been reviewing some people's concerns over rising wages.] The answer seems at first sight abundantly plain. Servants, labourers and workmen of different kinds, make up the far greater part of every great political society. But what improves the circumstances of the greater part can never be regarded as an inconveniency to the whole. No society can surely be flourishing and happy, of which the far greater part of the members are poor and miserable. It is but equity, besides, that they who feed, cloathe and lodge the whole body of the people, should have such a share of the produce of their own labour, as to be themselves tolerably well fed, cloathed and lodged.[13]

Were anyone to think these are just the observations of old men who are irrelevant these days in the United States, she or he has not been paying attention to the rampant poverty and consequent social anger in our cities and decaying countryside.

The Occupy Wall Street movement sees it and may push us somewhat toward an enlarged democracy, but the interests of the timocrats and oligarchs in opposing democracy are very strong.

Through the decades American liberals have come in a succession of forms, but our conservatives have been always pretty much the same. Long before the Tea Partiers, conservatives have regularly led the party favoring strong and aggressive military power, often without even giving it a mission—a sort of "my country right or wrong" attitude—and the party of laissez-faire economics. Its adherents are inclined to regard themselves as the real, mainstream Americans. Over time the conservative party has come to mean the one serving the oligarchy and the party of much patriotic symbolism.

In days gone by our traditional two parties and the system grown up around them, though they had a legion of faults, nevertheless helped to achieve some great things. For instance, the world has lived and foreseeably will live in the knowledge that existence itself is problematic. A grand accomplishment of our twentieth-century years has been that war among the European powers, the classic cockpit of war-making, has become almost unthinkable and there seems to be a good chance this will remain. Bipartisan foreign policies have underwritten that tremendous historic development.

An even grander accomplishment of our political parties has been that—no matter how stupid, corrupt, rotten politics around the world are—somehow THE BOMB has not dropped, somehow nuclear war has as yet been avoided. The country that made nuclear war possible, that did once embrace it, has not done so again. Generally, I have been a critic of American security (so-called) policies, but through bipartisan efforts we have led the world in seeking to deter nuclear warfare. The frightful explosion of six of Japan's reactors in March 2011 has driven humankind once again to realize the awfulness that could await.

In so many of its features this is a better world than our ancestors left us. If Democrats have led us in wars during the past century, Republicans led us into depressions. Not only the great one of the 1930s but the panics that plagued our pre- and post-Civil War nation and the recessions of our later years, including the "Great" one bred by our contemporary ruling class and from which we have not yet escaped.

I still have a vivid boyhood memory of my newspaper route in 1931 or '32. I had it for only a month, hawking Baltimore's least popular paper, the old *Post*. Every day my route brought me, about 5-5:30 P.M., around the corner of the Maryland General Hospital where a breadline cowered nightly. I remember my young realization that my own father might not be far removed from the men shivering there, though as yet the boarding and rooming house that my mother ran added a measure of sufficiency to his own wage.

In later years I could not recall that the breadline included any Negro men. God knows where they were eating. And later I learned too that the most devastating poverty of those Depression years was among the African Americans in our South, and it was starkly shared by the poor whites in our South who were all the while ruled by the most conservative, and in truth the least self-reliant, faction of the Democratic Party.

The war that the Roosevelt administration led us in fighting in the

1940s was in its run-up strongly opposed by millions (including my twenty-year-old self), but for a virtually united America it became the nation-defining event of our modern history. For good and for bad, World War II is the mother lode of all we now call the American way of life. Despite the distractions caused by the plague of Red Scares, the basic unity of the society held and was made firmer by the civil rights movement of the 1950s–'70s. Democrats and Republicans in those postwar days could at least tolerate each other. Is that commonality a thing of the past?

Whether the Tea Party movement lasts and whether the Republican Party continues its ascent in the near-term, I fear that today's aggressive conservative forces, servants as they are of the oligarchs and the military, are here to stay. I cannot suppress doubts that these forces can be entrusted with the mammoth responsibility of carrying our nation forward in a direction consistent with the values upon which the country was built.

IT IS TIME FOR the Republican Party to return to the old partnership of "nation building," of moving forward "a more perfect union." Our society will not return to its historic white unity. It will, by all indications, go in a quite different direction, as its values are formed, in at least equal measure, by women of all kinds and ethnics of many varieties: "black and white together, we shall overcome," we once sang and believed. What is happening is the point; and what is happening is that we are all, the many millions of us, becoming world subjects, if not yet world citizens.

One thing those old conservatives I earlier quoted had in common was that each and all knew that government is necessary. So too did the makers of our Constitution. Their purposes were expressed by active verbs: "form" a more perfect union, "establish" justice, "insure" domestic tranquility, "provide" for the common defense, "promote" the general welfare, "secure" the blessings of liberty, and "ordain and establish" this Constitution.

These were practical men. They were not afraid of action, of forward motion. The men and women succeeding them need to be as practical as they were, knowing that to govern is to confront needs and problems that reason describes and to cope with them. If we North Americans and Europeans have forgotten our knack for making nations out of our many selves—E Pluribus Unum—of being citizens and not mere pawns of bigger forces, then tragedy has begun.

And if so then our beloved republic will have to find for itself some minor role in a new world.

9

Our Unfinished Union

The American electorate of these late years has pulled back the shades on a nation of quick-changing moods and opinions. The election of 1968, one of the most dramatic in our history, followed the smashing Democratic Party victory of 1964, a landslide so overwhelming that it appeared to certify the Democrats as the nation's standard-bearer for years to come. But a mere four years later Richard Nixon would go to the White House.

In President Johnson's time we were going to build a Great Society. It did not happen, though a good start was made, until the war in Vietnam, as wars are able to do, choked it off. With President Obama's victory in 2008 and the giddiness of its promise of "Yes, We Can," we turned our heads once again away from awareness that the United States at its core is not a resolutely liberal civil or political society. We do in fact tend to be a nation divided just about equally between the two parties—the one of Franklin Roosevelt and the one of Ronald Reagan—and that is a wide divide though larger perhaps in outcomes than in concepts. The political tides of the 20-teens seem to be making it wider yet.

I have in my files a thoughtful reminder of that 1968–69 time. It is Walter Lippmann's January 13, 1969, *Newsweek* column written after the inauguration of President Nixon, and it said in part the following:

> Almost everyone agrees that there is a strong tide of reaction running in this country today. The critical question is just what the reaction is against and what it is for . . .
>
> The reaction is, of course, a conglomerate made up of views as far apart as those of Eugene McCarthy and Curtis LeMay [younger readers might want to substitute the names Rachel Maddow and Sarah Palin].

But there is, I dare to say, a common element. It is disappointment and anger that what was promised has not been delivered. The wide spectrum of the reaction is not against the good that has been done or has been reached for, but against the promises and the expectations that have been excessive and unrealizable.

Only on the fringes of the American people are there extremists who would retreat into isolation or go forward with hydrogen bombs; only on the fringes are there men who want the poor stopped from rising into affluence and a good life. There are not many who wish to imprison the blacks in a permanently servile caste.

He went on to mention promises and expectations arising in the Wilson and FDR administrations and from those of Truman, Kennedy, and Johnson, with also a sour look at Dulles's effort to encircle the Soviet Union. He labeled as "pernicious bombast" JFK's famous inaugural speech by which we committed to "pay any price" for the advancement of liberty.

It is cruel to raise hopes so high and then to dash them against the rocks of reality. Much of the bitterness in this land comes from the feeling that solemn promises of peace, affluence and harmony have not been fulfilled, and that evil conspirators must be at work and be the guilty ones.

The exaggerated promises have upset the normal human willingness to accept the fact that there are no sudden, that there are no universal, remedies for the hardness of the human condition on this planet.

A dose of Walter Lippmann hurts no one. His view about our situation at the start of 1969 is sound caution for us in 2012. Have we been easy marks for impossible dreams? But Lippmann in his final sentences, which I have omitted, did what in our politics is so commonly done. He turned away from reality in favor of hope. He expressed a bit of confidence that under President Nixon things might turn out better.

Under Nixon the nation settled down to Republicanism, relieved by four years of mostly marching in place with Carter and eight with

Clinton, good men both. It turned out, however, that the true victor of these Republican presidencies was the 1964 loser, Barry Goldwater. The Republican Party became his, more than Reagan's. He, more than anyone else, has been its political mentor, its economic guide, and above all its spirit and moralist.

The road since 1969 has had a quarry full of "rocks of reality" and many ditches, too, in which disappointments have often drowned. There were many measures of bright hopes along these years, similar to those recently unleashed by Mr. Obama in 2008, that crashed against what Lippmann called the hardness of the human condition on this planet, though, as Dr. Pangloss might say, it has been nevertheless better than many other possible presents or futures. Many of the broken ambitions could hardly have been anticipated or avoided. The United States is being twisted about by several social revolutions, from both the right and left, resembling earlier pivotal years such as the 1848 times in western Europe. Those too were times of world upset and deep change.

One such world change has been the political eruption in the Mideast, which neither governments nor "experts" expected. Who today, in the early years of this second decade of the twenty-first century, is bold enough to foretell how that extraordinary region will look a decade from now, or even a year from now? Of one thing at least we can be sure: statesmanship will be tested continuously. It will also be a near-certainty that the European and North American states will find their powers and influence in the region greatly diminished.

The United States enters this new era at a low point in its political history. At this time, we have no clear view or understanding of our self. Only foggily knowing our own minds and interests, we are, in our present condition, poorly fit to lead or even to act with consistency.

Of late, discussions of foreign policy have often dealt with whether we should be engaged abroad in "nation building" or in "regime changing." These discussions begin with recognition that some particularly weak or "failed" nation state is somehow incomplete, incapable of steering itself, and needing new leadership in order to redirect itself. Failed states are also seen as treacherous bogs that can entrap other states. My belief is that the ranks of unfinished states may now include the United States itself.

We are an older brother among democracies but not among political societies. We are the most notable among those polities that first gave itself a constitution and then later a nationality. We are a political "nation of the book." We could have stayed in Great Britain's embrace and then evolved like Canada, Australia, or South Africa. But instead we declared independence, secured it by battle, and proclaimed by law that we had created of ourselves a nation with promises to keep. We have lived that way ever since. Faithful to the Statue of Liberty, we gave hope to millions of the world's poor. From the very beginning of our statehood we have been aware that we have the tremendous challenge of constructing for ourselves "a more perfect union."

It has been a hard and perilous task. It was so in early years when a lot of New Englanders came to doubt the union was worthwhile. Then in the 1830s South Carolina, led by the charismatic John C. Calhoun, proposed to "nullify" a disliked federal law. Another Southerner, President Andrew Jackson, opposed and stopped that imminent schism. About thirty years later, when comity between North and South broke fatally following three weak presidents, Lincoln accepted and fulfilled the call he heard to preserve the Union. The cost for doing so was the horrible Civil War in which six hundred thousand were killed and the whole South, from Texas to Virginia, was forced into long-lasting poverty. A hundred and fifty years later it is not fully clear which side won.

The South has retained a hard core of its separate political identity. It has believed in the directions given it by the prophets of the "New South" in Reconstruction times, and has set itself to making money, as hard-nosed as a cast of Dickensian characters. It still is the poorest section of our country, though that may be changing; its economic road upward will likely continue. There is immense distance between its rich, who have always ruled, and its multitude of poor who, to the wonderment of outside observers, docilely for the most part follow them politically as they always have done and do so now into the Republican Party.

But such may not, for a lot longer, be its predestined future. Its economic structures and points of view continue to be shaped by the national economic powers. This present day "South" speaks proudly its political distinctiveness, while carrying water for Wall Street. For long it was an economic colony of the North, and still is to an extent, but now a proud one, having accepted in full the Republican gospel of wealth and having learned to excel in its practice.

The supply of Civil War anecdotes, authentic and spurious, seems endless. One I remember reading somewhere tells of a Union soldier in the final days of the gruesome Petersburg campaign, making captive a raggedy and hungry Confederate he had come upon, and saying to him as he points his rifle, "Gotcha!" To which the Johnny Reb replies, "And a hell of a git you got." Looking at the congressmen (mostly) that the Southern states send regularly to Washington, now as they did in the Strom Thurmond and Jim Eastland days, the git looks hardly better.[14]

We are too close to the days when the eleven Southern states waved the banners of "massive resistance" and "interposition," to have any excuse for forgetting them. That is especially so as the tide of Resistance has splashed from our Southern shores onto other regions and states. When in 1956 nineteen Southern senators—all but Lyndon Johnson of Texas and Estes Kefauver and Albert Gore of Tennessee—and 82 Southern representatives proposed and signed the "Southern Manifesto" of resistance to the Supreme Court's school desegregation decision, the Union itself was being questioned. I am not at all sure that in the intervening fifty-five years the spirit of estrangement has been overcome or even lessened. The bloc voting that I can remember old-school Southern politicians warning against, when they excited their constituents with the hobgoblin of supposed dangers if blacks voted, is a reality this half-century later; it is, however, bloc voting by Republican legislators, led by their Southern members, that may strangle American democracy in the twenty-first century's early years.

In the period following the Supreme Court's grand action of 1954–55, asserting the primacy of the Constitution over state laws that required the segregation of school children by race, the South plunged the republic into the necessity of defending its own legal order. That included protecting the lives of its people from the guerilla actions of violent lawbreakers throughout the region. We tend to remember those decades proudly as being the years of the civil rights movement and the heroic leadership of men such as Martin Luther King Jr. and Thurgood Marshall. And well we should. It was also, we should not overlook or forget, a period of defiance of the republic's law that should "live in infamy."

Abraham Lincoln memorably said that a nation couldn't live half slave and half free. True enough. Our present day question is whether it can live well, or well enough, half modern liberal and half non-liberal.

Liberalism in contemporary politics is defined by its bundle of convictions. They include

— an acceptance of the rightfulness of each person to membership in this society, which is made up of a diverse lot of recognized groups of people, all with a claim on our government that requires its respect and its defense of their "rights" as one of its primary purposes;

— a belief that all persons are entitled to fair chances for attaining economic well-being, and that our central government is duty-bound to give help to them as needed;

— a passionate belief in the openness of our culture to ideas, including new ones and their expressions; and

— a belief in the power of science and in defending its integrity.

I suppose more could be said of liberal values, but I think this is enough to characterize how different they are from the opinions of "nons." In the state where I live, one reads in the newspaper regularly of some officeholder announcing a shift from the Democratic Party to the Republican, invariably saying that she or he is doing that because the Democratic Party has become too liberal, is no longer the party it once was (meaning prior to the civil and voting rights acts of 1964 and 1965, though they don't say that).

Here is a close approximation of what they really mean but don't spell out (because to do so might mobilize the voting African Americans and the white "moderates"): we want it known, they are saying, that the South has accepted civil rights, that is over and done with, but we believe in the free enterprise system, we stand against "liberals" who want to weaken it by high taxes and more regulation, we have to protect our

Southern family values, and we must always be militarily strong and on guard against "radicals."

Our political life, and no longer only on the national level, is astraddle. Great Britain has long lived with its Irish divide and, in recent years, has loosened the constitutional ties of the Scots and Welsh. Canada has peacefully, and at its own chosen pace, defined the relationship it wants with London and has coped with the status claims of its French-Canadians. Where stands the United States' commitment to a "more perfect union?" It seems almost a certainty that, over the next decade or so, our citizens will be relocating themselves through some process on the valuation they give to national unity.

In the years since the legislations and the elections of the 1960s, party division has tended to solidify: Southerners like being together, in thought and in action. In fact, has there not been some returning to the conservative fold by, for example, the once deviant states of Kentucky and Texas?

Throughout the South, however, some outstanding universities will be, I would think, an undigested liberal culture and a force for unity. Somewhat ironic, perhaps, but the bond holding the region together may be its campuses. But let us for the moment suppose that the political divide continues, even deepens. How will that affect our lives, our non-political lives? Republicanism is so extremely restive on so many fronts with American liberalism that some deep change must occur, I'd think.

The "social" issues, as they are often referred to, are troublesome in our politics now and may get worse or be reincarnated in some other forms. I do not, however, believe that they have the potency to be a long-lasting cause of disunity. An important factor in today's society is that no matter how loud and belligerent our political controversy becomes it has not reached down to the fundamentals of what we like to call our free enterprise economic system. On those fundamentals we are so far united, more so than Republicans contend. We have no true "class struggle." There is no cleavage comparable to the nineteenth century's divide between an agricultural and a mercantile section.

The wealth of some and the lack of it of hordes more may finally, however, prove too great for the national unity's survival, but we are not there yet. With timocracy and oligarchy as the present controlling, ruling classes of our society, however, there may be ahead a time of reckoning when the classes recognize where they stand in relation to each other. And then the ties that bind us as a nation may fail.

The more immediate test will be of the Constitution itself. How much longer, for example, will we accept a distortion of our principles of "representative government" by suppression of majority rule in the Senate in favor of three-fifth majorities without formal change of the Constitution (shades of Calhoun!)? Every step away from our founding principle of majority rule, except in ways our founders prescribed, is another step toward oligarchy.

Another issue is the virtual repeal of the Constitution's unambiguous stipulation that going to war requires an Act of Congress. This is what democracy insists upon. Defying the War Powers Resolution on the theory that it is not invoked by our aerial bombardment of another country if no one is likely to shoot back at our planes is a triumph of war-making over law.

A third is the enlargement beyond any good sense of the number of presidential appointees who must receive Senate confirmation. Democratic government requires that elected officers be able to govern.

And a fourth is the need to monitor the powerful appellate courts, most especially the Supreme Court which has, session after session, enlarged its own power. Personally I do not believe that the Court's historic record justifies its members' lifetime tenure when the Constitution only provides that they shall serve during their "good behavior." If there was any truth at all in Chief Justice John Roberts's statement during his confirmation hearing that his job is like a baseball umpire's, just calling balls and strikes, then it's not a hugely intellectual post. The real truth is that the roles of the justices are intensely political, and have been ever since John Marshall. Cases routinely turn out with votes split along party or ideological lines. It is disingenuous to pretend otherwise. Thus, even a hard-working garbage collector could have accurately predicted the outcome of *Bush v. Gore*. Ten years on the bench ought to be enough to protect and insure a justice's independence.

These are Constitutional issues that should trouble us greatly. There cannot be a well-functioning democracy without power to act legislatively, and that cannot be without a clear path to majority decisions, which is not true now. The government has to be able to make up its mind, and to act. As it is and has been, our Constitution is already replete with checks and balances and protections of minorities; we don't need more. The majority has rights, too. Further concessions to the South, which essentially is what the sixty percent rule is, amount to a radical revision of the Constitution.

I have noted the alterations within the United Kingdom whereby Scotland and Wales have pressed for and have gained some governing powers. In England, the Conservative Party now in office is looking ahead over the next four or more years of its term to finding new ways to deliver wanted services through nongovernmental organs, a movement away from what it sees as a "too big government" and toward "Big Society." Conservative parties are in ascendancy in many countries including, of course for the moment, the United States. The future is opaque, though one thing has again been made emphatically real: genuine democracies, depending as they do on the restless populace, will have both conservative and liberal sides in almost equal measure. Democracies are continually afire, often aflame, often smoldering; but they must be able to act.

I would like to believe that the progress in our times toward gaining racial and sexual equality will be lasting, I think it may be secure, even from reactionary conservatives, mainly because it is self-fulfilling; emancipated persons can and will defend themselves. I would like to believe that world colonialism as known from about the fifteenth to twentieth centuries will not reappear, though the cancerous effects of it are likely to get worse. I want to believe that the concerns for our natural environment to which our centuries have given birth will continue their growth and will not be defeated by their inevitable conflict with the oligarchs. I feel less confidence regarding the most necessary of all endeavors of our times, escape from the culture of militarism and war; they have been humanity's most grievous sins against itself.

That this congenital sin still among us affects more of us than ever is simply because there are more of us than ever. It is also because of the profits to be made from arming us with ever more extravagant weaponry. Probably, at least possibly, we can feel a smattering of confidence that, in the late twentieth century, Europe got well from its ancient habit of warring within itself and that we have lost our appetite for more territories (at least on Earth). But Europe still exports armaments for other governments to employ, and we do the same on a much larger scale.

I offered above a plan for peace, and I restate it here:

Stop honoring our warriors so strongly. Stop accepting warring, and the preparation for warring, as being the natural and necessary essence of our nation. Free our minds from that, in order to confront, better and more directly, civilization's challenges.

* * *

That you are patriotic will be praised by many and easily forgiven by everyone; but in my opinion, it is wiser to treat men and things as though we held this world the common fatherland of all.

— DESIDERIUS ERASMUS

As I write this, another Memorial Day has come and passed on. In another two months we shall have our next patriotic holiday. It is not, however, the martial celebration that Memorial Day is and that Veterans Day in November will be. Our 4th of July seems to be still what it was meant to be: our national birthday party, complete with cake and ice cream and candles and some parades and fireworks.

I think it is good that we have a national holiday to commemorate our wars, the fighting of them and the bravery of the men and women who died. I am less understanding of the whys and wherefores of Veterans Day. It seems rather redundant. Until recent years on November 11 we observed Armistice Day—the end of the World War. But then we had another and bigger World War and there was no Armistice that could be believed in. Almost right away we embarked on warring without stop:

Korea, Vietnam, the Cold War. Congress, unwilling to give up memorializing, created Veterans Day. It was, if you think about it, conceptually almost the opposite of Armistice Day.

None of this warring appears in retrospect to have achieved whatever it was we intended. Many would say that the Cold War, because it extinguished the Russian "threat," was a success, but we are left with a recklessly capitalistic Russia while we ourselves flounder economically.

Memorial Day's oratory was about bravery and how our wars have defended and even created our freedoms. Those of us who think wars have done no such thing mostly keep quiet. There are always, it seems, some good souls who speak up, saying things like "let's honor our soldiers by bringing them home alive," but generally except in greenhouses of liberals they do not get much audience.

From the depth of a segregated United States, where he couldn't get a cup of coffee, and in the midst of the Great Depression, Langston Hughes hymned:

> Let America be America again,
> Let it be the dream it used to be . . .
> Let America be the dream the dreamers dreamed
> Let it be that great strong land of love
> Where never kings connive nor tyrants scheme . . .
> O, let my land be a land where liberty
> Is crowned with no false patriotic wreath
> But opportunity is real, and life is free
> Equality is in the air we breathe.[15]

During the War the United States would celebrate "I Am An American Day." I do not recall that custom, but, had I been in Central Park in New York on May 21, 1944, to hear the day's chosen speaker affirm his faith, I would have. It was the distinguished jurist Learned Hand. In his brief address he said:

> What do we mean when we say that first of all we seek liberty?

I often wonder whether we do not rest our hopes too much upon constitutions, upon laws and upon courts. These are false hopes; believe me, these are false hopes. Liberty lies in the hearts of men and women... What then is the spirit of liberty? ... The spirit of liberty is the spirit which is not too sure that it is right; the spirit...which seeks to understand the minds of other men and women; the spirit... which weighs their interests alongside its own without bias; the spirit of liberty remembers that not even a sparrow falls to earth unheeded.

At this conclusion, the judge led the assembled patriots in saying the Pledge of Allegiance.

On the question of whether it is possible to emancipate humanity, or at least portions of it, from the ancient curse of killing our neighbors, I have proposed that, in first one then another locality or community, we stop honoring military service so richly. Or possibly in one nation and then another would do likewise. Is that contrary to human nature, whatever that is? Once, and it was not long ago, we were told that the South would *never* accept integration. Well, it did. Did it not? There have been other unexpected mind shifts in our evolution. One was accepting despite our senses that the Earth is round and spins around the Sun instead of the reverse. A good maxim might thus be: in the affairs of human beings, rule out no possibilities.

10

FRATERNITY

Those of us whose lives began in the 1920s have had quite a ride. We missed the Great War but little else of the historic horrors that dominated the early years of the century and set the direction and challenges for the decades to come. One of those challenges—atomic weaponry—mankind may be fated never to escape.

Some survivors such as myself look about for signs of what may be ahead in the onrush of time. My own perhaps astigmatic view is that future generations have some high ground to build from, and defend. The peak of our time has been the expansion of our democracy in amazing ways, accomplished much more quickly that I and many others would have believed possible. African Americans, women of all colors and races, Mexican Americans and other Latinos, native Indians, Asian Americans of several strains, all are being brought inside the tent. Not far enough inside, they would likely say, and that battle will also continue here and around the globe far into the future.

That fine Italian philosopher Benedetto Croce spoke of "history as the story of liberty," by which he meant that the really important happenings are not the wars and tragedies of human existence but the progressive realization of humanity's rich abilities in science, arts, morality and political understanding. I am open to believing that, though the despoilers of civilization can and do wield mighty power, they can be overcome. It is grimly true that the political challenges faced in the last century were so awful, so basic, that no defeats could be accepted or endured. The same may be true for the generations ahead.[16]

Democracies are seldom tranquil. Class struggle is the essence of democracy. It has been so since at least the days of classical Athens and Rome, maybe even of Cain and Abel. No ruling class has ever been immune or safe from it for long; or should be. Struggles for rights and powers are at the heart of democratic life. In democracies, class struggles can be practiced peacefully. That is one of the reasons democracies are good.[17]

A family story has it that I tagged along behind my father to the polling place where he held me aloft as I voted for fellow West Virginian John W. Davis for President in 1924. Davis did not get many votes and might have been grateful for mine. The next time Mr. Davis got my attention, he was a noted Wall Street lawyer and the lead attorney for Clarendon County, South Carolina, in the great case that became *Brown v. Board of Education*, which struck down segregated-by-law schools. For him, and the South he then represented, it would be a deserved loss. It was a vital chapter in "the story of liberty."

The most precious right we have is the vote. Its exercise has always evidenced class struggle, or, said differently, strong disagreement about competing economic interests. In this twenty-first century the Supreme Court has weighed in mightily on the side of the rich. Even compared to *Scott v. Sanford* (the Dred Scott case) and *Plessy v. Ferguson, Citizens United* was one of the most destructive decisions in our judiciary's history. It gave corporations unprecedented influence over federal elections.[18]

In the *Federalist Papers* we are asked, "Who are to be the electors of the federal representatives?" And the answer given is, "Not the rich, more than the poor; not the learned, more than the ignorant; not the haughty heirs of distinguished names, more than the humble sons of obscure and unpropitious fortune. The electors are to be the great body of the people of the United States."[19]

But when one with normal intelligence reads the struggling and cloudy opinion of the Court in *Citizens United*, and then reads Justice Stevens's powerful dissent which leaves the majority opinion in shreds, one can hardly doubt that the Court's decision, from start to finish was to "give cover" to the result they wished to reach: that money in unlimited amounts should be able to flow from the most powerful interests into elections, creating super-electors. Nowhere in the founding documents is there a suggestion that the Supreme Court should have any say in choosing electors at all, and to base the decision on the First Amendment is a distortion of its purpose.[20]

The grand and glorious First Amendment is not a super-Constitution and should not be stretched out of shape to serve as one. Freedom of speech is but a mere abstraction if it is not proclaimed in service of the people—allowing them the freedom to speak their minds on political questions. Invoking it to enable corporations and the wealthy to dominate the political process and to stifle the voices of the people strikes at the heart of democracy.

So, is this where we are now, at the juncture of timocracy and oligarchy, with liberal democracy clinging on? But shakily? And for how long? Could it survive another world depression?

Our statesmen have sometimes called the United States the indispensable nation. Is that because we are lovers of liberty, the keeper of order, the disinterested wise patron? Or is it because we are the protector of the wealthy?

The inequalities that abound among the world's peoples could hardly have been expected to last quietly. When, in our own nation the Occupy Wall Street movement had available to itself the slogan "We Are the 99%," referring to the reported gulf between the wealth controlled by the wealthiest one percent of us and that by the rest of us, it is talking about a division that simply will not be allowed to last, or else our democratic republic has lost its muscle and inner spirit.

Had *Plessy* not been overturned, the result would have been the development of a national system of apartheid on the South Africa model. If *Citizens United* stands for long, if indeed corporations are "us," then I wish the "99%" all success in finding chinks in the corporate system.

Discontents will almost surely overwhelm the status quo. The grossest inequality is between the richer industrial economies and those that exist on the margins of the world's economy. And it is almost impossible in our time for any people to live outside the large economy, unless perhaps in the deepest jungle. This is one world.

Disrespect for wealthy corporate powers is no longer rare in our press, as such had been but a short time ago; that is a good thing. In the 1960s, it had been my perception that there would be no decisive break with the segregation system of the South as long as it was beyond open public discussion—and there was not—and that it would not last beyond the time it was put on the defensive in the public media. And it did not. I doubt that timocracy and oligarchy in their present dimensions can last a whole lot longer.

Which means, I think, that there will be lots of unrest in our near future, here and in the other societies of the world where there is large private wealth held by a small minority. And I think that, as formerly with reforms of the 1930s and of the mid-'50s, the '60s and '70s, the time for unrest has arrived, like it or not. Racial segregation, as existed in the United States up to the 1960s, or in South Africa, was incompatible with modern economies, cultures, and levels of education.

The same can be said of contemporary oligarchy. My guess is that oligarchic societies will have more lasting power than did merely racist ones and that reform of them will take longer. After all, the equalitarian reforms in the United States required only change that did not go very deep. If revolution means changing the ruling class, we have not yet had one.

Another great urgency is rethinking the military's life and role in this democracy. Can any thoughtful person really believe that incessant growth of armed "missions," of weaponry and the continual invention of new ones, of the constant devouring of treasure, all of this life of destruction, is good and sustainable? I think not, but I think also that finding a turnaround opportunity will be terrifically difficult. Did those "Cold War" Pentagon budgets seal our destiny; can we escape from them?

If ascendant conservatism were to succeed in stripping the domestic agenda of social programs, what else except warring would be left for the national government to do? The conservative party seems to have little or no use for investments in education, public health, or the arts. It wants to reduce the national government to "protection of the people." What would that mean but more war and military spending?

War remains for states an expectable way of achieving desired political results. The Kellogg-Briand pact proposed by the United States in 1924 would have renounced, or outlawed, war as an instrument of national policy. It was signed by nearly all countries, including Germany and

Japan as well as by the United States—led at that time by a Republican administration. It went into effect on July 21, 1929; then everyone, despite it, resumed arming.

There is no clear exit from a culture and practice of militarism and its gluttony. When our constitution proposed "to provide for the common defense," can that mean creating "commands" led by viceroys that encircle nearly all the world and involve us in the internal affairs of other governments? But God is good, and our merciful sustainer. And if history is truly the story of liberty, i.e., of human life, perhaps better days do lie ahead though now hidden from our sight. If true, there will still be jobs to be done if ours is to be a well-functioning government—as it now is not.

We Americans are engaged, first of all, with our permanent question: Can this be truly home for all our people? Democracy is a big tent, as I have said above, and in that respect it is synonymous with America itself. We are the land of big tent democracy. Our manifold faults are democratic ones. Our manifold high qualities are democratic ones. Being such has been this country's function, as it were. Our watchword has always been "freedom." Some of our teachers, like deTocqueville, have thought that we might need to protect it from the other ideal we have had, that of equality. I think the two must now and in the future stand or fall together. The present and future demands within democracies are for equal opportunities, as "equal" is defined by the citizenry. We are in the process of learning that "we" are indeed one people.

The old trilogy was liberty, equality and "fraternity," and the third I think may be chief of all. Fraternity is the demand made by all religions, but unlike liberty and equality it is not enforceable by law. Instead it is a call to find our own way of living in sisterhood and brotherhood with those with whom we share this time and planet. There is no more worthy ideal.

∽

NOTES

1. An outstanding book is Barbara Ehrenreich's *War*, Henry Holt, 1997.
2. *The Ruin of J. Robert Oppenheimer*, Priscilla J. McMillan, Penguin, 2005. See also *American Prometheus*, Kai Bird and Martin Sherwin, Knopf, 2005.
3. While my direct involvement with the military had ended with my Atomic Energy Commission days, there was still to be my family 's confrontation with the Selective Service System during my son's four years of contest with it, seeking to be recognized as a conscientious objector during the Vietnam War; finally he won, just as the draft ended. And there were to be my own efforts beginning during the sordid Vietnam War to oppose it. Mine were not momentous actions. They did, however, lend support to the gathering forces that would by 1975 yank us out of that war. I had a close working relationship with an organization known as the Center for Defense Information and another called the Center for National Security Studies of which I could be called founder. CDI still exists and is an important part of the Washington array of citizens' peace groups.
4. Matthew 22:2; Mark 12:17; Luke 20:25.The wording in the three synoptic gospels is virtually the same.
5. 554 U.S. 570 (2008).
6. *U.S. vs. Miller*, 307 U.S. 174 (1939)
7. Vintage Books, 1991, pages 90–91.
8. *The Republic,* Book VIII, pp. 545-553. Which is the best translation of all this I am not the one to say, but the one richest in interest may be the old Jowett one.
9. Robert Michels, *Political Parties,* translated by Eden and Cedar Paul, The Free Press, 1949; page 383. As his career closed Michels joined Mussolini's National Fascist Party.
10. In another book, Michels seconds Vilfredo Pareto's theory of "circulation of elites." "This theory, briefly, maintains that no association can do without a dominant class, but that the dominant classes undergo rapid decay. At first they become enervated; then they experience a process of dissolution; finally they morally and physically succumb . . . to a new dominant class that arises from the people. The people as a collective never can democratically govern itself, but the rulers themselves change continually." *First Lectures in Political Sociology*, University of Minnesota press. 1949, page 63.
11. *Politics,* Book IV, 1295b-1296a, translated by Wm. Ellis, edited by E. Rhys, Everyman's Library.
12. *Aquinas, Selected Political Writings,* edited by A. P. D. Entreves, translated by J. G. Dawson, Blackwell-Oxford, pp.81,135,137
13. *The Wealth of Nations,* edited by Edwin Cannan, Modern Library, pp. 78-79.

14. See the author's *The Shame of Southern Politics: Essays and Speeches*, University Press of Kentucky, 2002.
15. Hughes, "Let America Be America Again," 1936.
16. ". . . when periods of barbarism and violence are approaching it is only for the vile and the foolish that the ideal becomes unfreedom and slavery; for others it remains that which alone can be called human, the only ideal which always works. We always tend towards liberty and work for it even when we seem to be working for something else; liberty is realized in every thought and in every action that has the character of truth, poetry and goodness." Benedetto Croce, *History as the Story of Liberty*, translated by Sylvia Sprigge, New York 1941, pp. 231-22. Truth, poetry and goodness are Croce's ethical categories.
17. It is worth remembering that it was Aristotle in classical Greece who first taught that a strong middle economic class makes for the soundest society and government.
18. *Scott*, 60 U.S. 393 (1857); *Plessy*, 163 U.S. 537 (1896); *Citizens United v. Federal Election Commission*, 558 U.S. 08-205 (2010).
19. *The Federalist Papers* Number 57.
20. Several methods of deciding how our representatives should be chosen are discussed in *The Federalist Papers*. One will find a lively awareness, by Madison in Numbers 57 and 58 and by Hamilton in Numbers 59 and 61, that care must be taken in this process, but one will not find any assumption or belief that the judicial branch is or should be involved in that.

ABOUT THE AUTHOR

L ESLIE DUNBAR was born in January 1921 in Lewisburg, West Virginia, one of the oldest towns in the state. He is descended from a long line of early Scot and German settlers and circuit-riding Methodist ministers. His family was an early victim of the Great Depression and left the Greenbrier Valley for Baltimore, where he attended public schools, including the University of Maryland. When the war came he worked at the Glenn L. Martin aircraft plant, followed by graduate studies in political philosophy and Constitutional law at Cornell University. In a career marked by broad interests, he has taught at Emory University and Mt. Holyoke College. He has been a Guggenheim Fellow and has held visiting appointments including the University of Arizona and Xavier University in New Orleans. In the early 1950s he was an administrator with the U.S. Atomic Energy Commission at its sprawling nuclear plant in South Carolina. In 1958 he followed what he called "the passion of my times" and joined the staff of the Southern Regional Council in Atlanta, the South's oldest race relations organization, and in 1961 became its executive director. During his tenure that Southern Regional Council was at the center of efforts to desegregate the public schools and secure passage of the Civil Rights and Voting Rights Acts, and oversaw the organization of the Voter Education Project which helped to registered more than two million African American and minority voters in the 1960s. In 1965 he became executive director of the Field Foundation in New York, with primary missions of improving child welfare and expanding civil rights. He was a research associate with the Ford Foundation before moving to Durham, North Carolina, where he was active in the social justice ministries of his church. He "retired" in 1987, and has continued to speak widely and contribute articles to a number of publications. He now lives in New Orleans.